11-12-05

To:

MARY,

The Best Neigbor
Guy could Ask for That
For The GREAT Memmories

WISHING

HAPPINESS

4 U

ALWAYS.

God Bless

Jeff Gotel~

The Visitor
Reveals the Steps
to Happiness

by

Jeff Ireland

authorHOUSE™

1663 LIBERTY DRIVE, SUITE 200
BLOOMINGTON, INDIANA 47403
(800) 839-8640
WWW.AUTHORHOUSE.COM

First published by AuthorHouse 09/20/05

ISBN: 1-4208-8661-4 (sc)

Printed in the United States of America
Bloomington, Indiana

This book is printed on acid-free paper.

Dedication

For – Arlene – Ashley

Kayla –Sam

Acknowledgements:

Thanks to Buck Thomas who has employed me for the best part of my career. He has allowed me to realize many of my goals and dreams including this one.

Thanks to Mark Wineka my editor for making my rambling story one that makes sense and one that is easy to read.

Thanks to my manuscript advisors, who took the time and effort to give me valuable feed back before this book went to print. Especially Dave who is the best 'human spell checker' I know.

Thanks to my Mom for all the years of support she has given me. No matter how goofy I got over the years she always believed in me.

Thanks to my siblings who through our relationships during my life have influenced the person I became.

Special thanks to Arlene who has always given me 100% support regardless of how crazy life gets. I would never be the man I am without her love and support.

Extra special thanks to Ashley, Kayla and Sam what can I say? They are the three greatest kids that any man could ask for. They, along with their mother have shown me and given me the greatest happiness a man could have here on earth.

Finally thanks to God for all of the blessings he has given our family to experience.

Table of Contents

"Happiness is a state of mind in which your
thoughts are pleasant the majority of the time"

- Maxwell Maltz

Prologue

As I turned the car into our subdivision, I thought everything was just as it should be.

It was about eight o'clock in the evening, and I was just getting home from work. I had been there since five that morning, but those kinds of days were normal and the price one had to pay for success, I told myself.

Sure, other people my age were as successful, but I was doing better than most. Driving past the neatly trimmed lawns of our middle-class neighborhood, I figured my life was pretty darn good. Not bad for a small-town boy from Lower Michigan.

I drove a luxury car, and my company paid for all the gas, too. Our stylish, comfortable house came with a swimming pool, something I had always wanted but my family could not afford when I was a kid. My own kids attended private school, and we had a motor home parked beside the house for our summer vacations.

It seemed like the things I wanted and dreamed of as a boy had come to fruition.

This lifestyle came, of course, with sacrifices. I worked hard and for long hours. And if I were honest with myself, we were probably in debt more than we should have been. But I was a young 46 and, besides, it was only money. That's how I rationalized it.

I had become a vice president of a large firm in Charlotte, N.C. Boy, what would they say back home? That thought kept playing in my head as I walked into the house and my wife, Arlene, said dinner was in the microwave.

"Dad, can you play a game with us tonight?" Ashley asked

"Yeah, Dad, we're playing Monopoly," Kayla said.

"Please, Dad," young Sam pleaded.

"I can't tonight," I answered. "I've got to go back in my office and get some work done on a project that is due."

"Aw, you are always working on something," Ashley complained.

"Honey, can't you play one game with the kids at least?" Arlene joined in.

They seemed to be piling on, and I lost it.

"I can't believe this!" I shouted. "Don't any of you realize that I do this for you, so you can have a better life and a comfortable life?"

I stormed down the hall to my office and slammed the door. I did not emerge until everyone else had gone to bed.

Didn't Arlene and the kids appreciate what they had and what I was doing to make sure they had it? I was only doing it for them, so they could enjoy the things in life I never really had back in Michigan. Yes, I knew I traveled too much and worked late far too often. I really didn't take great care of myself, given that work was a bit of a pressure cooker. But that came with being a vice president. Didn't they see and understand that?

I knew I had skipped a few recitals and maybe a school thing or two. So I missed a first step or first word. The kids will take and say plenty more, I said to myself. Work took top priority for now. It's how we paid the bills. How we kept up. How we stayed happy.

Still with all this so-called success of mine, all the material things and the impressive job title, did I have it all? I felt a longing for something that seemed to be missing.

How could my life be so full and all-consuming, yet still have an emptiness to it?

Chapter One

Tragedy Strikes

The voices seemed to float in from a dense fog.

"Oh my God, it's 64 over 50!"

"Quick, get a different bed!"

"Slide him over to this one."

"Throw away the pillow. It's soaked clear through!"

"How could you let this go this far without telling someone?"

One nurse kept repeating something.

"Jeff, keep looking at me. Don't you go back to sleep again!"

I sensed they were taking me someplace else, as their voices kept weaving in and out of the fog.

I was in NorthEast Medical Center having my second heart attack in as many days. The first one occurred the night before. It's something difficult to describe. It hurt, yes, but not the excruciating pain I would have expected. I had entered the hospital emergency room about 10 p.m. and waited until 4 a.m., when they put me in a room. At that time, the doctors saw no evidence of my having a heart attack, but they were keeping me a day for observations.

That was Friday. I had been awake for about 22 hours straight and had been poked for tests at 4 and 8 a.m., I was tired and, needless to say, very cranky. Once I had my wits about me, the first call I made was to my wife, Arlene. She wanted to know everything the doctors had told me. The last she had heard from me was when I left the house with chest pains and drove myself to the hospital. It seemed like a big inconvenience at the time. I gave her the basic information before starting in.

"Man, am I upset," I told her. "Do you realize that I have an appointment for lunch today?"

"Who is going to cover my work?"

"Do you realize they did not find anything yet"

"I told you it was a false alarm."

"I've been awake all night trying to figure out what our deductible is."

My harping continued. Arlene patiently waited for a chance to speak, finally asking if she should bring the kids to the hospital or take them to school.

"Take them to school," I said. "This is nothing more than a false alarm, but damn, am I upset."

She told me she would visit after breakfast and sit with me awhile until doctors performed the stress test. As I slammed down the phone I heard a scuffling noise.

A small man, bent with age, busied himself near the door to my room. He had round shoulders, frail hands and silver hair, but he moved quickly. I judged him to be in his late seventies or early eighties.

"Just here to pick up the room," he said. "Don't mind me, although I will say you seemed a little sharp with the missus considering your condition and all."

"What do you know about my condition, old man? You don't know anything."

"Well, I actually know quite a lot from my first look at you," the old man said. "Let me see, you are way too young to be in here for heart trouble, which is what your chart says. You most definitely should not be yelling at your wife, because you were missing an appointment. Plus, I would say you appear to be in good shape otherwise. "All these things tell me you're too busy chasing the rabbit to pay attention to your blessings."

He shook his head, as if in pity.

"Chasing the rabbit?" I shot back, sitting up a little higher in my bed. "What in the world are you talking about, old man. And besides, what do you know about my blessings?"

"For starters, I know you're still alive, and you apparently have a wife and kids who care about you," he said. "And the name is Elmer, but they call me 'Grandpappy.'"

He moved back toward the door.

"I wish you luck," this man, Elmer, added, "and maybe I'll see you again during your stay." He waved as he left.

"Kooky old man," I mumbled to myself. "Chasing the rabbit. What was that all about?"

Within an hour Arlene and the kids had arrived by my hospital bed. I continued my ranting about how I had wasted a night and how I was going to miss the day at work. The doctor walked in soon and, in a matter-of-fact tone, informed me that the blood work had come back. I most definitely had suffered a heart attack. The next steps were to schedule me for an angioplasty, a procedure in which the doctors would insert a tube and expand a balloon to open up my clogged arteries.

I must admit, the emotions came rushing at me like a freight train. I felt terrible for being upset with Arlene for making me travel to the hospital in the first place. Now I was lying in the hospital with her and the kids beside me, and my worst fears were being realized. This seemed the most unlikely of outcomes, considering I was only 46 years old, slim and in excellent shape from chasing the kids around.

The night before, I had just come from coaching two basketball practices and running up and down the floor with the kids. Naturally all of the questions came with the emotions: How bad was it? Was there damage to the heart? How would it affect my health? How about my job? Oddly enough, when I posed that last question to myself, I thought of what the old man said. "Chasing the rabbit."

The angioplasty took place at 1 p.m. Friday. By all measures, I thought it went well, and everybody told me it was a routine procedure. Line 'em up and flush 'em out, Just like an assembly line. Finish one, scrub up, prep another, do it again. My procedure went fine. They cleared out two arteries and put a stint in another to keep the artery open.

The afternoon went by slowly. I wasn't allowed to move off the bed, or even lift my head. I had to lie still for eight to nine hours to give the artery a chance to heal. I couldn't read. I couldn't even get a good look at the room's television screen. I had to lie perfectly still with my head flat on the pillow.

Because I came out of the procedure at 2 p.m., I had to lie there until 10 p.m. All this time, I kept hearing the old man say "chasing the rabbit" and pictured him shaking his head back and forth. What did he mean?

By the time I was able to get up and move, all of the family had left. My sister, Denise, had taken the kids, and Arlene had gone home to bed for some much needed rest. The nurse came in about 10 o'clock and told me I could get up and move around, much to my delight. But when I moved, the trouble started. I heard a faint pop and felt a very sharp pain, which shot through my leg straight to my brain.

The pain was like nothing I had ever experienced in my life. It was constant and getting worse. I rang the nurse's bell. She responded quickly enough, but she told me I was probably just stiff.

"I know stiff, and this is not it," I said loudly. "Something is bad wrong!"

"Not to worry," she said. "It will go away shortly." She left.

Within minutes I was ringing the buzzer again and telling her much the same thing. I received the same answer and response.

Things went from bad to worse. I started to sweat profusely, and the pain started in my chest. To complicate matters I was hyperventilating. The only way I could seem to get air was sucking on my drink straw with no drink in the glass.

I rang the nurse's station one more time.

"I am telling you something is bad wrong, and I think I am going to pass out." I said.

In a rather snippy voice, she asked, "Have you ever passed out before?"

"No," I yelled, "but I am telling you I am in pain that I have never felt before and I am sure I'm having another heart attack!"

"Calm down. I'll see what the doctor on call has to say."

She stormed out of the room.

The pain worked up the right side to my stomach. I was not sure what was happening, but I knew for certain I was dying. As I lay there on my side, grabbing the side bar on my bed with all my might, I prayed.

"God, forgive me of my sins, and please take care of Arlene and the kids. If it is my time, I am ready. Please, just take the pain away."

God answered one prayer almost immediately. The pain went away when I became unconscious.

Then the voices I mentioned earlier came floating out from the fog, taking me to the intensive-care unit at NorthEast Medical.

The rest of the night was touch and go. The automatic sleeve on my arm took my blood pressure every twenty minutes. I had an oxygen tube going to my nose and, in my other arm, a feeding tube and nitrogen tube, mainlining the drug to keep my heart calm.

I found out later that my chances of survival that night were fifty-fifty. I improved rather quickly, and I don't believe I ever really comprehended how grave my situation was. But there I was, drifting in and out and asking for pain medicine every three to four hours. On Saturday they took me downstairs for more testing, which confirmed my suspicions from the night before.

I had suffered a second heart attack. The first was mild to moderate; number two, moderate to severe. The pain that was so devastating the night before originated from the artery in my leg, where the doctors had inserted the angioplasty tube. Somehow the artery had torn, allowing my blood to seep out into my body.

I ended up with hemoglobin (basically a pool of blood) that settled between my stomach and kidney. It measured 10- by 20- by 6-centimeters in size, or the equivalent of two pints of blood. I had almost bled to death from the inside. I found myself alone again on Saturday afternoon, somewhat hazy from the medication, when the old man walked into my room for a second time.

"Well, well, if it isn't my old buddy, the rabbit chaser," he said. "Heard you had a pretty rough night there, young fella."

I thought I detected some genuine warmth and concern.

"Yeah, you could say that again, Elmer," I said, still detecting some sarcasm in my voice.

"From what I hear, you're pretty lucky they caught it when they did, or you might not be talking to me today. You'd be chasing that rabbit in the sky. And please call me 'Grandpappy.' Everybody else does."

"Yeah, that's what the doctor says, but you know I'm in pretty good shape and pretty tough to boot."

"All you rabbit chasers think that, but it sure would have been a shame if you had bought the farm and never really understood the meaning of true joy and success."

"Oh, and I suppose you know? And what is this rabbit-chasing business you keep talking about? That just makes no sense." I was getting testy.

"The rabbit chaser? I learned about it over eighty years ago from my father, but it would take me about thirty more years to actually figure it out. Now I have studied this for a long time, and you are definitely spending too much time chasing the rabbit."

"I know you think I'm one," I said. "You have been telling me so since I first saw you. What I want to know is, what is it?"

"A rabbit chaser is a man or woman who chases the dream that they believe will make them happy and successful but they are mistaken. They think success and happiness come from material possessions, position, job titles and such, and that is just plain wrong. So many people believe in the old adage, the one with the most toys when he dies wins."

"If you're so smart give me an example of a rabbit chaser," I demanded.

He smiled. "Let me tell you the way I learned," he said.

"Charles Schwab, Edward Hopson, Arthur Cooger, Cosabee Livermore. Do any of those names ring a bell?"

"No. Not really, except for Charles Schwab has that investment company" I answered.

He shook his head. "Not the same man," he said. "Young man, back when I was growing up, the most important thing was money and nice things, important jobs, that sort of thing. These men were household names at the time, you know, the Roaring Twenties, and my father told me then that they were all rabbit chasers. Now how could that be, I wondered. Presidents of giant companies. Famous money handlers. Some of the most successful people of that time. I never knew what he meant exactly. That is why it took me thirty years to figure it out."

"What happened to them?" I asked. "How did you figure it out?"

"Well, let me give you the run down:

"Charles Schwab was president of the largest steel company in the world at the time. He ended up dying a pauper.

"Edward Hopson was the president of the largest Gas Company in the world back then. He went insane.

"The president of the New York Stock Exchange, Richard Whitney, went to prison and was released just in time to die at home.

"Arthur Cooger was the greatest stock speculator the country had ever seen. However, he died abroad, penniless.

"And ol' Cosabee Livermore, known as The Great Bear of Wall Street, committed suicide."

As he spoke, my medicine kicked in, and I started drifting off to sleep. I thought I heard Elmer, er, Grandpappy, say something about the end of today's lesson.

Soon, I was dreaming. I was sitting at my desk, hard at work. Every time the blood pressure machine would kick in, a truckload of dollar bills fell from the ceiling and saturated my office floor, turning it into quicksand. As I worked away and the money was covering me, I could see Arlene and the kids looking at me through a glass window, trying to reach me. They couldn't. I reached out to them, but the dollar bills kept covering me. As I tried harder and harder to get out from under the money, I sank deeper into the quicksand. The money buried me and my desk. I wanted to be with my family, but all I could do was continue working.

Each time the phone rang a rabbit also started running around the room. I was afraid the quicksand might suck up the rabbits, so I tried catching the critters to protect them.

I was chasing rabbits as my family tried desperately to save me.

Chapter 2

Taking Care of Business

Waking up, I noticed that my wife was sitting in the chair beside me.

I smelled like medicine, I thought. Sterile.

"Hey, Beautiful," I said.

"Scary night last night," she answered. It was both a statement and a question.

"Yeah, it wasn't one of my best. The doctor says the worst is over and the internal bleeding has stopped. That is a major accomplishment."

"They are coming back this afternoon for some tests, and we will see what that tells us," Arlene said.

Her voice had a frailty to it, and I could tell she was on the verge of tears.

"Where are the kids?" I asked, trying to change the subject.

"Denise and Jim took them to lunch and out for the afternoon."

"How are they doing?"

"Fine, but confused and I think a little scared. They want to know why they can't come and see you in this part of the hospital."

Now she changed the subject.

"How was your morning? Did you sleep the whole time?"

"Well, good, and no, I didn't sleep the whole time. I had a visitor that was interesting."

"Interesting? How so?"

"Have you seen this old man running around? I think he is a volunteer named Elmer, but they call him "Grandpappy.""

"No, I haven't. What does he look like?"

"Old, probably in his seventies or eighties, but very spunky and talkative. A little bit annoying, too."

She shrugged.

"He was here this morning, jabbering something about being a rabbit chaser," I said. "You ever hear of that expression?"

"Yes, doesn't it mean someone who is chasing money or material things and who works a lot to do it?"

"That is what he said," I answered. "Do you think I am that way?"

"I would definitely say you are driven. Why don't you get some sleep and stop worrying about it."

I eventually went back to sleep. When I woke up again, Arlene was gone and Grandpappy was in my room.

"Hey there, Grandpappy." I was actually glad to see him.

"Hey, yourself, young fella."

"So Grandpappy, do you have a way to provide for my family and live in the lifestyle we are accustomed to, other than chasing rabbits?"

I was only half-kidding.

"Of course. I never thought you'd ask. You know, you do not get to be my age and able to do the things I do without a system. To me, 'lifestyle' is a subjective term, up for various interpretations. Life will put you at different stations as you mature and age. The key is to appreciate where you are and what you have with an attitude of understanding and acceptance.

"Also, what you might find if you adjust your expectations is that the lifestyle you have is a lifestyle your family never really wanted anyway. What they really wanted was you and your time."

"I guess that makes sense," I said. "So, do you share your system with people, or is it a secret?"

"It certainly is not secret and, quite honestly, it is pretty much common sense. The key is what order you place the habits and how much emphasis you put on them that make the difference. I don't necessarily go around talking about my system and don't teach it, unless a smart young fella like you asks."

He smiled.

"The 'habits,' as in plural?" I asked. "How many habits are there?"

"Ten for the basic plan that will put you on the road to peace of mind, happiness and success."

Be careful, Grandpappy, I thought. You're suddenly sounding like a motivational speaker at a business conference. Still, I felt like taking the bait.

"Well, when can I start learning this system of yours?" I asked. "That is, if you would be willing to teach me?"

"To be honest, you have already had your first big lesson two nights ago and then got an even bigger dose last night," he said. "Health is the first big key to my system and the cornerstone of my philosophy to true success and happiness."

"Health?" I said. "Are you serious?"

"Actually I am. Let me ask you: Last night, when you were having a heart attack and bleeding internally, were you worried about the 401(k) or the stocks in your portfolio? Of course not. Were you worried about the next big sale or if the office girl showed up for work on Monday? Nope.

"Think about when you get the flu or a bad cold or maybe you have allergies. Do you really feel like a pumped-up, motivated, dynamic, self-starting, goal-setting, hard-charging individual? Of course not.

"Without health, you lose the ability to focus on the other steps. A feeble body acts powerfully on the mind and is a clog to its progress. Health is essential to enable us to succeed in life. If you lose your health, you also lose the desire to achieve and be at peace with yourself."

"Shoot, Grandpappy, look at me," I said. "I am healthy, and I'm lying here with a heart attack. Doesn't that blow a hole in your theory?"

"No, not really," he said. "You see, you are not completely healthy. Look at all human kind, way back into history. Nothing has been so persistently sought as a healthy body. Now people think that a youthful looking body is a healthy body, and that's not so. Now we realize that good physical health starts in the mind with good mental health.

"Yes, I would agree that on the outside you appear to be healthy, but you're not. How could you be? You have had two heart attacks at the age of 46. What is unhealthy is your thinking. What you need to understand is, you need to expel from your mind thoughts and images of death, disease and all discordant emotions, such as hatred, malice, revenge and envy. Bad thoughts, just like bad food, bad drink or bad air, make for bad blood. Positive, healthy thoughts are essential to healthy bodies.

"As a man thinketh in his heart, so is he." It is such an important component to health and vitality, it cannot be overstated.

"There is an old Chinese proverb that says, 'He who sows hemp will reap hemp; He who sows beans will reap beans.' You need to transfer your thinking from the negative to the positive plane. Think only healthful thoughts, and speak only healthful words. Let the thoughts that are uppermost in your mind, whether you are alone or with others, always be those thoughts that make for health, strength and power. If we could cultivate the habit of living our lives on the plane of the positive, not in the realm of what we fear or dread or doubt or distrust, our susceptibility to sickness of all kinds would largely disappear."

"You're not suggesting that health is mental?" I said.

"No, but it is the essential start. Good food and a good balance of it is very important, along with plenty of water to wash out the impurities in your system. There are so many diets and ways to approach eating, I really could take a year talking about them all, but here are some basics that work for me.

"Once you have your mind right, simply eat in moderation. You might try this method: The Ed Forman school of thought is, take in twenty-five percent of your caloric intake at breakfast, fifty percent at lunch and twenty-five percent at dinner. Throw away the salt shaker and the sugar bowl, and you got it covered. Remember to always drink plenty of water. You just can't get enough of that.

"Another thing to keep in mind, something you can't go wrong with, is the old Jack LaLane diet. If God doesn't make it, don't eat it. It just doesn't get any simpler than that.

"Other basics you may want to know: Fruits and vegetables have colors. When a vegetable or fruit has lost its color, it has lost its value. You should always eat fresh and ripe fruits. Students of nutrition say colorful foods are rich in vitamins and mineral salts. Red vegetables, tomatoes, strawberries, radishes and apples are energizing and vitalizing.

"Yellow foods, such as corn, squash, carrots and sweet potatoes, are rich in life elements.

"Green foods, like watercress, spinach and other green, leafy vegetables and tops of many plants are generously eaten by anyone who studies foods for health.

"You are what you eat and what you drink and, let me add, it is what you digest, assimilate and circulate in every cell, nerve, tissue, root and fiber of the entire body that counts."

According to Grandpappy a person also needs to add in some good cardiovascular exercise. Nothing complicated, he said, just a good aerobic routine and a lot of brisk walking will do the trick. He was making sense. I hope he didn't think I was bored, but I couldn't keep myself from yawning. Darn it, I was falling asleep again. It had to be all the stuff for pain they were pumping into me.

"Grandpappy, I think you made some valid points ..."

I'm sure I didn't finish the sentence.

As I slept, I dreamt I was lying in a bed of gold and jewels. I was sick and not sure why, but I knew I could not get out of the bed of gold. I had tubes going into my body and a nurse standing by me shaking her head. I was on the phone talking business with someone. The tubes were pumping money into my veins. As I looked up, there was fruit hanging from the ceiling that I could not reach. I wanted that fruit. As I looked over to the other side of the room, I saw my family on treadmills, walking at a brisk pace and waving at me. I kept talking business and the money continued to come down the tube into my veins. I waved at them but could not get out of the bed of gold to join them.

I sat up and yelled, "No more." As I tried one more time to reach the fruit on the ceiling, the dream went away.

Chapter 3

It's in the Mind

I drifted in and out of sleep for the remainder of the day. Arlene came back and spent the afternoon and evening with me. We talked about how fortunate I had been that things were settling down, and I told her all the things that Grandpappy had shared with me.

"I don't know if I would be listening to a volunteer or not," she said, a bit scolding. "I think you should be consulting a doctor about your health."

"I'm not saying he has all the answers," I said, "but he sure made it sound pretty simple."

"That's my point," she said. "It all sounds way too simple, and I just don't think it can be that easy."

"Don't you think we complicate life sometimes? You know all of the pressure we put on ourselves? It's like the old song says, "Why is it so hard to sit in the yard and stare at the sky so blue?" I think our society in general can't sit still and just appreciate what we have."

Arlene probably wondered what fool notions this "Grandpappy" was pumping into me along with the pain killers. The look on her face said Grandpappy might be a nut case. Possible, I thought. But a tolerable nut case.

Arlene went home to get some much needed rest. The kids were staying with Denise and Jim for a couple of days. We thought it would keep their minds off me and help the whole situation.

The tests had shown little improvement in my red cell blood count. It looked like I was going to remain in intensive care for awhile.

I had a fitful night. The nurse gave me a shot for the pain at one point and, when I woke Sunday morning, Grandpappy greeted me. Doesn't he ever go home, I asked myself.

"Preaching about health again today?" I asked.

"No, I'm not, and I don't think I preach at all. If you recall, you asked me if I knew of a better way to live, and I told you I did. I don't think I came in preaching."

"I'm sorry, Grandpappy. You're right. I just had a bad night, and my whole world is upside down. I guess I am a little depressed."

"Apology accepted. Now, would you be interested in learning the next step?

"Sure. I have nowhere else to go, and what do you mean by next step?"

He sat down next to my bed.

"One of the keys to becoming happy and successful is to build a positive outlook," he said. "Many people call it a positive 'attitude,' and some people just call it 'attitude.' I like to call it a 'can-do attitude.'

"There is an old Latin expression that when translated says, 'He can who believes he can.' Or put another way: If you think you can, or if you think you can't, either way, you are right."

"Yeah, Grandpappy," I said, "but I know better than to live in a Pollyanna world where everything is great all the time. That is just crazy."

"No, you're not getting my point," he reprimanded. "Look, everything starts in your head. You would think that a farmer's insane if he threw or sowed thistle seeds all over his farm and expected to reap wheat. But we sow thoughts of fear, thoughts of worry, thoughts of doubts and anxious thoughts. It's no wonder that we are not in perpetual harmony.

"The harvest from our thoughts is just as much the result of law as that of the farmer's sowing. Seed corn can only produce corn. A man's achievement is the harvest, big or little, beautiful or blighted, abundant or scarce, according to the character of the thoughts he has sown.

"A man who sows failure thoughts can no more reap a successful harvest than the farmer can get a wheat crop from thistle. If he sows optimistic seeds of harmony, health, purity and thoughts of abundance and prosperity with confidence and assurance, he will reap a corresponding harvest. Likewise, if he has thoughts of failure, despair and poverty, that is what he will attract into his life.

"A person who would take a knife and begin to slash himself until the blood flowed would be put away in a mental ward. Yet we are always slashing our mental selves with sharp thoughts. We use tools such as hatred, revenge, anger, jealousy and fear, and yet we think of ourselves as normal and sane. You've heard how we try to describe ourselves at times: 'I'm just a little high-strung or maybe edgy,' are the words we use.

"Jeff, what I am talking about here is a law where there is no guesswork. 'Like must produce like.' It is impossible for it to work otherwise.

"Am I getting through? Is it making sense?"

"Yes, I guess it does," I answered. "But, you know, I can't go through life without problems and challenges."

"No, of course not," he said. That stuff happens to everybody. That is not what I'm talking about. I'm talking about how you handle the things that happen to you. Excuse me just a moment. Maybe I can explain it better for you."

He left and came back in about two minutes with a flashlight.

"Grandpappy, are you planning on the lights going out?" I said, chiding him a bit.

"No, I'm trying to get one to go off in your head," he said, as he unscrewed the flashlight's cap and removed the batteries.

"Jeff," he said. "This is a flashlight." He held it up in the air.

"Yeah, one with no batteries," I said.

"Exactly," Grandpappy said, satisfied that he was on the right track. "This flashlight represents your life. And, of course, what does it take for the flashlight to work?"

"Batteries," I answered.

"Exactly. Now the batteries represent energy, correct?" I nodded.

"OK, let's take one of these batteries. It has two ends, one positive and one negative. This battery represents the things that will happen to you in your life. Those things will be either positive or negative or somewhere in between. The things that happen to you in life, you may or may not have control over, correct? Your heart attack, for example."

"Yes, I guess so," I said.

"The second battery represents how you handle those things that happen to you. The way you handle things is the same as the other battery. You can be positive, negative or somewhere in between. Whether you realize this or not, there is but one thing on this earth that God gave you complete control

over, and that is your attitude. You see, your thoughts are your attitude. That is what I have been trying to tell you. You have the ability to control your thoughts to be either positive or negative."

He pushed the batteries back into the flashlight. But he put the second battery in upside down.

"If you handle things in a negative way then the light will not work," he said. He demonstrated that the light would not turn on.

He removed the second battery and replaced it correctly.

"If you handle things in a positive manner, it will allow you to shine the light, your light, on other people.

That, Jeff, is what God intended. He wants you to shine the light of your life on other people. You need to listen to Jesus in John 8:12:

'I am the light of the world; he who follows me shall not walk in the darkness, but shall have the light of life.'

"All I am telling you is, you need to follow His example with confidence and help light the way for the people in your world. Attitude is everything, as everything stems from it. As I say, it's the only thing over which you have 100 percent complete control. God planned it that way for a reason, because He knows it truly is the only thing you need to achieve success and happiness.

"Look, bad things will happen and leave you in a fog of fear, doubt and worry in your life. The trick is to get rid of it and deal with it in a timely fashion. I like to use the 'fog analogy.' A seven-square-mile area of fog, when it is condensed down, is the equivalent of about a half glass of water. And, of course, there's the glass of water example you've always heard.

"If you are optimistic, you would say the glass is half full. If you are pessimistic, the glass would be half empty, right?"

"That's what they say," I answered.

"Well," Grandpappy said, "I think they're way off. The question should be, 'How heavy is the glass?' You see, that all depends on how long you hold the glass. If you hold it for a few minutes, it is not heavy at all. If you hold it for an hour, you will start to lose focus on what you are doing, because it will take all of your effort and strength to hold the glass. If you try to hold it all day, you would end up here in the hospital

"So the trick is to dump out the water and get out from under the fog of self doubt, fear, worry and stress and move on with a positive attitude. The first step in dealing with adversity is to look at it and acknowledge it. All I am saying is, approach life with a positive attitude and learn to shine your positive light on other people."   I could tell he was finished with the morning lesson.

"I will leave you for now. Rest well, my friend."

I dreamt again. I was in the woods on a foggy night. I was trying to find Arlene and the kids. I held a flashlight that would not work. I took out the batteries and noticed the batteries were in wrong. I replaced them with the positive side up and continued walking slowly ahead. My light was shining on hundreds of people all around me, yet I could not see their faces.

I was trying to shine my light on others, but I still was not finding my way or my family.

Chapter 4

The Twin Pistons

By mid morning Sunday, not much had changed. The pain remained a persistent companion. I was still grouchy. And even my visits and talks with Grandpappy, who I kept reminding myself was only a hospital volunteer, had left me dazed and confused. Also, I told Arlene, I was a little bit impressed with the old guy.

Arlene perked up. Wasn't I the one who said earlier that Grandpappy was a crazy coot?

"Is he telling you about health again?" she asked.

"Not just that. He seems to make more and more sense the longer I talk with him about life," I said. "It's odd, but I think I am really connecting with him.

35

He made a very interesting analogy about life being a flashlight and the batteries being the things that happen to you and the attitude you take toward them."

By now, Arlene didn't know how to react to my talks with her about this mysterious old fellow whom she had yet to meet. She changed the subject quickly to the kids and all of the people from work and family who had called to see how I was doing. Plenty of flowers and plants were going to the house, which pleased Arlene, who could have been a horticulturist in a different life. Our house in the winter looks like a greenhouse and, in the spring, our yard resembles a Disney cartoon, thanks to all the color from her different plants.

When my lunch came, it was the usual uneatable hospital food, the kind they insist is nutritious. What would Grandpappy say about hospital food, I thought.

After lunch, Arlene went off to the store to prepare for the kids coming home. Denise and Jim were bringing them back home this afternoon, and Arlene said the refrigerator was pretty low. I was watching a basketball game on television when I heard Grandpappy's now familiar voice through the curtain.

"That game worth watching?" Grandpappy said without looking up at the screen.

"Not bad, I suppose," I said. "I'm not really rooting for anybody. Just killing time, and I'm not in the mood for reading."

"Well, if you're not going to read, why not take another step toward the good life on your road to success and happiness?" he asked.

"Oh, right, and I am just going to jump out of bed and do that here in the hospital?" Even I didn't like my sarcasm. But Grandpappy smiled back.

"Yes, that would be the idea," he said.

"How exactly would you recommend I do that? I suppose it is another one of your secrets for happiness?"

"You seem to be missing the point," the old man reprimanded. "It is not a series of secrets. It is a philosophy with ten distinct steps to it and, yes, this would be one of those steps. In fact, it is two steps in one. I like to call them the 'twin pistons' that drive the human spirit."

"All right, Grandpappy, I'll bite. What are your twin pistons that drive the human spirit?"

"I wish I could take the credit, but they are not my twin pistons. They are God's, and they are what He would want you to discover and use to better fulfill your life."

"Here we go," I protested. "Are we going to make this a church service?"

"There you go with that bad attitude again," he scolded. "Let's just put it this way, you are put here on earth to succeed and to achieve, which will result in happiness and success. Purpose and planning are what the twin pistons are. With them you can achieve anything, even things that seem impossible to you now. Without them, you will be destined to wander through life without aim or purpose."

"Men and women achieve the best results in every department of effort only as they thoughtfully plan and earnestly toil in a given direction. Purposes without work are dead. It is foolhardy to hope for good results from plans alone. The purposes of successful people in business and life are always followed by careful plans to reach those goals. It has been said that 95 percent of people wander around aimlessly; taking what life hands out and not realizing that with a little planning and a lot of determination they can get out of their rut and soar to heights never dreamed of. Did you know a rut is only a grave with the ends kicked out?

"So do you have goals, young man?"

"Of course, I do. Everybody has goals. We all want something more in life."

"Do you have your goals written down anywhere?" he asked.

I looked away from him and answered sheepishly, "No, not really."

Grandpappy was adamant on this point.

"Look," he said, "if your goals are not written down so you can read them, they are just hopes, wishes or dreams. They're not really goals.

"Jeff, you have to write down the things in life you want to have and do. You see, your mind can only hold one conscious thought at a time. That thought is usually on the task at hand, not your dreams for the future. You need to plant the thought for the future and the things you want in the form of a written goal in order for your subconscious to understand what you want it to do. Your subconscious is the fuel which drives the twin pistons.

"Your subconscious does not know the difference between a penny or a million dollars. It does not know the difference between success or failure, and it will work just as hard to achieve one as the other. It is up to you to decide what you want for you and your family. You must tell your mind, 'This is what I want and I am willing to work toward that goal.' It says in the Bible, 'As a man thinketh so is he. And in the book, 'Think and Grow Rich,' by Napoleon Hill, it says, 'We become what we think about.'"

"Grandpappy," I said, "I have never done it the way you are describing. All I would do is write down something?"

"You could do it that way, but I prefer a systematic approach," he said. "First of all, when you write your goals, make them smart goals."

"I don't think I would make them stupid, Grandpappy," I said, pleased with my joke.

"No, I don't mean it that way," he said, ignoring the feeble attempt at levity. "I am saying SMART as an acronym. The 'S' stands for 'specific.' You have to be very specific when asking your mind to work on something. The more specific the better. The 'M' stands for 'measurable.' You have to have a measure on your goal so you will know when you have achieved it. The 'A' stands for 'action.' Many people will write down goals and throw the list in a drawer and not make any action steps toward the intended purpose. You must take action toward your goal. The 'R' stands for 'realistic.' You cannot set ridiculous things as your goals and expect to accomplish them. For example, it would not be very realistic for me to become the heavyweight champion of the world in boxing. Now that is an extreme example, but I think you get my point. The 'T' means 'timely.' Put a time frame on what it is you would like to accomplish. Once again, it needs to be realistic. And don't be discouraged if you don't obtain them all. Put it on next year's list."

"Hold on, Grandpappy," I said. "I just don't get you. First, you tell me I am a rabbit chaser and that I should not chase money and riches. Then you tell me I need to write down what I want and what I should work for. Well, I have three small kids so, of course, I would have goals of making money so I can send them to college and pay off our house. Now how can I do that without setting goals to make money?"

"Again, you're not getting my point," he said. "I never said money was bad. You have to have it to survive and to buy things. My point was not to worship money nor spend every waking moment trying to make more of it. Set realistic expectations and work toward them. Put some faith in God, and trust in Him that He will provide for your needs. Not only will He provide for your needs, He will lead you on the right paths to achieve the goals you have set. It says in scripture 'Seek ye first the kingdom of God and all other things will be added unto you'."

"I am still a little confused," I told him.

"Let me tell you a little system I have used for many, many years that has served me well," he said. You may understand what I am talking about a little better. I like to separate my goals into categories or groups. I use the word 'spirit' as a guide to help me to remember my system. It also reminds me that goals are the force that drives the human spirit. And the subconscious is the fuel that drives the force. Again, it's an acronym.

"But first, as I tell you about this system, I want you to understand that you are not in competition with anybody. Set the goals for you and your family, and don't compare yourselves to other people. Too many people do that. Compare themselves and what they possess to other people. One of the big problems in the world today is that too many people compare their insides with other people's outsides. They think of all the adversity, turmoil and strife we go through on a daily basis and compare it with the masks that other people wear. The masks say, 'Look what I wear. Look what I drive. Look where I live.' They see the material wealth of others, and they want the same. Many people will borrow and go into debt far beyond what they can pay back comfortably. We live in a world where our wants prevail over our needs. Don't get me wrong, it is OK to want nice things and desire to go nice places. The problem comes when we borrow to achieve these wants because we want them now, and we lack the discipline to save for the good things in life. Young people want what their parents have and more right now. That's the problem. They compare themselves to people who have worked twenty or thirty years to achieve and acquire possessions and build a comfortable life and they want it now. The system will help you keep things in perspective while you build your dream life.

"Let me stress again that 'the good life' is not about acquiring material goods. It is most definitely about how you live with an attitude of purposeful joy.

"Each letter in the SPIRIT formula is the first letter of a category in which you will set three goals. The letter 'S' represents spiritual goals. You should always have at any given time three spiritual goals you are working on at all times. This category is very important to the foundation on which everything else is built. Ecclesiastes 2:26 says, 'For [God] giveth to a man that [is] good in His sight wisdom, and knowledge, and joy: but to the sinner He giveth travail, to gather and to heap up, that he may give to [him that is] good before God.'

"If you do not have a strong spiritual foundation, you are in for a long road of misery indeed. The next letter, 'P,' represents professional goals. As I told you earlier, money and career are not the problems if they are handled correctly and kept in perspective. When your career happens to get in the way of your family life, or if it forces you to go against your spiritual beliefs, it is not worth the job or the money.

"It is a tough balancing act, however, it can be achieved if you work at it and desire it. Many people get caught up into the old trap of, 'Well, I must work a lot to give my family the things they want.' This is nothing more than a cop-out, covering up the things they really want to have. Many others will work from the argument that, 'Well, yes, I spend a lot of time at work, but the time I spend with my family is quality time.' Quality time is not something you can manufacture or just decide, 'OK, now we're going to

have quality time.' Quality time comes unexpectedly when the time, place and company are right. The only way to get quality time is by spending quantity time. It cannot be stressed enough: Time is one thing you'll never get back. So as you plan your professional goals, be sure you carve out ample time and save room for the next category, which I call the 'institutional family.' These 'I' goals are the most important because, as you set and achieve things as a family, you are actually building the character of your kids. You are building and molding their young and impressionable minds with experiences and confidence that will last them a lifetime. Also, as you plan and complete your family goals, you instill in them the desire to be a part of your life as you reach your golden years.

"There are two things I never want you to forget as you raise your kids:

"One, your kids may not hear what you are saying, but they sure do watch what you do. Another way to say it is, 'Your actions speak so loudly I can't hear what you are saying.'

"Two, Lead by example.

"The 'R' stands for retirement. Some day your working life will be behind you. It will be different for you and your family when that time of your life arrives. It is imperative that you plan to support yourself in old age. The current government retirement system will not be as it is now, when you're ready to use it. You must plan for that. It will be much better in your golden years to know what you are planning and have the means to live those dreams out. If you want to know what to plan for, take a look at yourself. What you will do in your retirement is what you do now in your spare time. After all, what is retirement but permanent spare time. That is why so many people retire and wither away. When the retirement party is over, they literally have nothing to do. Some start jobs or hobbies. Many just give up and die of boredom.

"The next category, in fact, is 'I' for 'interest' or hobby goals. It is imperative if you are to become a well-rounded person to have things you enjoy outside of work and family.

"The last of the categories is 'T' for travel goals. With the world literally at your fingertips, where do you want to travel? Many of these can obviously roll back into blended family or retirement goals, but you should be working on a specific travel agenda now. Travel expands your breadth of knowledge, and I encourage you to take the long boat to China, so to speak.

"Just like working toward a goal maybe more pleasant and rewarding than actually achieving it, the same holds true for a trip. The journey is half the fun. Whitman says the journey is better than the inn, and this is very true more often than not. I encourage you to explore our great country and world. It is now more available than at any time in the history of mankind, and be sure to do as much as you can with your family. Remember, quality time comes from quantity time."

Grandpappy made me repeat the system to him before he said goodbye. Before he left the room, I picked up a sheet of paper and pencil. On the sheet of paper, I wrote down the SPIRIT system and left room for three goals under each heading.

S.M.A.R.T.

S.P.I.R.I.T.

Spiritual

1. _____

2. _____

3. _____

Professional

1. _____

2. _____

3. _____

Institutional family

1. _____

2. _____

3. _____

Retirement

1. _____

2. _____

3. _____

Interest (Hobby)

1. _____

2. _____

3. _____

Travel

1. _____

2. _____

3. _____

I was worn out. I dozed off again, this time with pencil in hand. I dreamt I was in a chair that was moving through my house, although I was not paralyzed or in a wheelchair. It was just a moving chair. I moved from one room to another, gliding and unable to get up or stop. When I went into my office, the room opened up into a great hall with twenty- or thirty-foot ceilings. The huge walls had paintings of treasures and scenery. They were all beautiful.

My chair kept moving through the hall, and I realized the paintings depicted my dreams and desires. My goals. But they were all out of reach. Under each painting, stairs appeared as I passed. The problem was, I couldn't get out of the chair to walk the stairs. On a distant wall, I spied a book titled, "How to Climb Stairs with Action Steps." I could never get close enough to grab it.

I simply floated down the hall with my dreams just out of reach. I didn't know how to take the first step toward them.

Chapter 5

Friend or Foe

Two things waited for me when I woke up: Arlene and dinner.

I had no complaints about Arlene. I couldn't say the same thing about the platter in front of me. Matted, pressed and formed turkey swimming in watery gravy. It looked like wallpaper paste. I think those were green beans and soggy carrots on the side.

A long way from Bob Evans, I thought.

I learned that Denise and Jim had volunteered to keep the kids one more night, since they could not see me in the intensive care unit anyway. I missed the children terribly. I told myself I was feeling better and was ready to try some walking.

This hospital stuff was wearing thin.

"They'll let you walk when the doctors say it's safe for you to walk," Arlene said, after I protested out loud. "Keep in mind it was only twenty-four hours ago you almost died. You need to slow it down and lighten up just a bit."

"I know, Honey," I said. "I am just upset and confused. I am trying to figure out how this happened and why. You tell me things happen for a reason, but this one sure puzzles me.

"I'll tell you, the only bright spot in the whole mess is Elmer."

"Who in the world is Elmer?"

How could she have forgotten so soon?

"You know, the old man I was telling you about who works as a volunteer here," I said. "Grandpappy."

"Oh, yeah, the man you saw yesterday."

"Actually, I saw him this morning again after you left. And we spoke for what seemed like a long time."

"That's funny. I asked the nurse when I came back if anybody had been to see you today, and she said it was pretty quiet."

Arlene had a puzzled look.

"Well, I'm sure they would not consider someone who works here to be a visitor," I said.

"You might be right. To be honest with you, I am surprised they would allow even a volunteer to be in here bothering you that much, considering the shape you are in

"Well, what did you two talk about this afternoon that took so long?"

"It wasn't much of a conversation. It was more of a long lecture about what he called the twin pistons that drive the human spirit."

I told her about purpose and planning and setting goals.

"Jeff, we set goals already. We have a whole host of things we want to do and accomplish. It doesn't sound like anything new or earth-shaking to me."

"Well, he made a good point. We do not have our goals written out on paper, do we? If it is not written out, it is not a goal. It's a hope or wish. He also gave me a "spirit" formula, and all and all, it was pretty cool . I want to try it as a family when I get out of here."

She agreed in theory and said she wanted to learn more.

About that time, Larry and Bryan from work popped in for a visit. They stayed until visiting hours were over. The Carolina Panthers had just won the National Football Conference championship, and the guys gave me a Panthers hat. I gave them a hard time for not bringing me tickets to the Super Bowl instead. They also brought me a Men's Health magazine, and we shared a good laugh at their sense of humor. Seeing I was in good hands, Arlene scooted out and headed for home. The nurse finally waved the guys out of there. ICU apparently has strict rules about visiting hours.

It wasn't long before Grandpappy came shuffling through.

I told him about the guys' visit.

"Hey, you know for a volunteer, you seem to be here a lot ," I said. "They apparently work you pretty hard."

"The fact of the matter is, they don't schedule me at all," Grandpappy said. "I just come around when I sense I am needed. I don't really work the whole hospital as much I seem to gravitate to a particular patient. You, Jeff, happen to be that patient this week. I hope you don't mind that I am visiting a lot, talking to you about my system."

"No, Elmer, I am finding it pretty interesting, even though I think you are outdated in some of your thinking sometimes."

I said it with a smile, so Grandpappy wouldn't be insulted. He wasn't.

"When you start thinking clearly," he said, "you will see that the steps I am covering with you are actually quite timeless in nature. Take independence, for example. It has been around since the beginning of time, yet it is taken for granted these days and people still do not understand its importance."

Independence. I wondered where he was headed with this one.

"I do not refer to the country's independence," he continued, "if that is what you are wondering, but independence and freedom from the burden of debt and financial stress.

"Debt has made more people miserable and disrupted the comfort of more homes than almost anything else in the universe. To do your best in life you must own every bit of yourself. If you are in debt, part of you belongs to your creditors. Nothing other than sin against God can be as paralyzing to young people as debt. Not a single person can do their best work, no person can express themselves in terms that commend respect and no person can either create or carry out a definite purpose in life with heavy debt hanging over his head. The person who is a slave of debt is just as helpless as the slave who is bound by ignorance or by actual chains. A man who is enslaved by debt has no time or inclination to set up or work on the things in life that create joy, happiness, fulfillment, self-satisfaction and respect. The result, then, is that he drifts downward with time until he eventually begins to set limitations in his own mind. He traps himself behind the prison walls of fear and doubt from which he never escapes.

"It is a terrible thing to think of going through life like a prisoner in chains, bound down and owned by somebody else on account of debts. Living in a prison of fear and doubt. The accumulation of debts is a habit. It starts out very small and grows to enormous proportions slowly, step by step, until it takes charge of one's very soul."

I stopped Grandpappy here.

"I understand debt and how that type of thinking may have been fine when you were young," I said, "but it is a different world out there today. With the taxes the government places on us. The need for two cars. And kids. They need more things than the kids in the old days did."

"Hold on there, Jeff. I can see where you are going with this and it won't wash with ol" Grandpappy.

"First, let's define "need" and "want." That is where the last few generations have crossed the line and allowed greed and desire and coveting what others have to take over for good common sense.

"Again, and hear me well. The problem with the world today is that too many people compare their insides with other people's outsides.

"You see, we live lives like everybody else. Everybody goes through adversity, turmoil and strife in their lives. Nobody is immune to these things (their insides) if you will. Everybody has problems, and a lot of them. Now some people have more money or more fame, but they still have problems. People go about their lives comparing themselves to the masks that other people wear, the side they show the world to say, 'Hey, look at me. I'm OK. Look at the car I drive. Look at the clothes I wear. Look at the house I live in' (their outsides). In the old days, we used to call it 'keeping up with the Joneses,' but today people have taken it to a whole new level.

"Now people want to keep up with the sports stars, the movie stars, and the extremely wealthy, of course, the only way the average person can do that is by going into debt. You couple that with the easy money that is available, the basic ignorance toward money and debt most people have, and you have the perfect storm for the blurring between need and want.

"What do we really need, and what do we have and do because of want? Need for a man and his family has always and will always be the big three: food, shelter and clothing. If we look at food on a per-person basis, the cost to feed your family as a percentage of your income is the lowest it has been in the history of mankind. Where it used to consume 35 to 40 percent of your income, you can now feed your family on less than 10 percent.

"Shelter? Well, more than likely, you will have to go into debt for that purchase. However, why not buy a house that suits your needs, not a small mansion just to impress your friends?

"Clothing? Once again, the cost of clothing is less expensive than it has ever been before as a percentage of income. The big difference here is the false value put on certain brands by the 'in' crowd (all of the 'outside' people). There is also status today put on where people shop to get their 'needs.'

"Take away those three essentials, and most people work from the notion that they 'need' material goods that actually they just want, to keep up 'outside' appearances."

Grandpappy stopped to determine if I was taking in any of his message.

"You have a point - well, actually, many good points, Grandpappy," I said. "But it is so hard in a society where things that were once luxuries are now necessities. Like a car, for example."

"Yes," he said, "but there is a big difference in cost between a used Chevrolet and a new Cadillac, and that is my big point. Yes, you need a car, but not the top of the line if you cannot afford it.

"Jeff, I know we cannot cover it all tonight, but think of two things: Stay away from too much debt. And save something out of every paycheck. It is critical to the person you will become later in life. You see compound interest can be either a friend or foe. It will work just as hard to make you rich by saving as to make you broke by borrowing.

"Andrew Carnegie once said, 'The first thing that a man should learn to do is save his money. By saving his money he promotes thrift - the most valued of all habits. Thrift is the great fortune-maker. It draws the line between the savage and the civilized man. Thrift not only develops the fortune, but it also develops a man's character.'

"Young fella, I cannot express the importance of this topic enough. Some of the finest qualities of human nature are directly related to the correct use of money, such as generosity, honesty, justice and self sacrifice, as well as the practical virtues of economy and thrift.

"On the other hand, there are the counterparts of deceit, fraud, injustice and selfishness, as displayed by the inordinate lover of gain. There are the vices of reckless spending and borrowing, extravagance and wastefulness, on the part of those who misuse and abuse the means God entrusted to them."

In my dream that night, I was shoveling snow from the walk in front of our house, and about the time I had it cleared away, it would start snowing again. I noticed a new car in the driveway. I almost cleared the drive, and it snowed again. When I turned around, the kids were running out to get into a new motor home sitting farther down the drive. The more I shoveled and felt as though I were making progress, the harder it would snow, getting deeper each time.

As I looked up into the sky I noticed a bank sign and under it a message board touting higher interest rates. There was a man looking down at me laughing, and I realized I was in a glass snow globe.

The man looking at me was the banker. He counted money while shaking the globe and covering me with snow. As I looked down, the snow turned to money, but the money was debt. It weighed on me like a mountain, and all I wanted to do was dig my way out. The banker was laughing.

Chapter 6

Don't Wait

I woke up in the middle of the night, ringing the bell for the nurse. She obliged with some medication, and I talked to her briefly about my new friend, Elmer.

She said she had never heard of him, although that didn't necessarily mean anything because she had worked in ICU for only eight months. He could be new, she said, promising to check on him for me.

Arlene had some good news in the morning. The doctors told her I could move to a regular room that day if my blood count returned to normal. After some small talk, including the news that the kids were coming home later, I abruptly changed the subject.

"You know, Honey, I think we should get ourselves out of debt, and I want to do it quick," I said.

"That's a great idea, Jeff, but what brought this on all of a sudden?" she asked. "You weren't talking to your old buddy, Granddad, or whatever his name is, were you?"

"It's Grandpappy and, yes, I was, now that you mention it." I said. "Is that a problem, or do you find that funny in some way?"

"No, not at all. I can't wait to meet this man. I have heard so much about him and his ideas that he is very intriguing to me. I think mainly because he seems to not only have great ideas but he seems to be getting through to you. I haven't heard an idea yet that I haven't liked. Maybe we should have him over for dinner some time."

My doctor soon arrived to report that my red blood count continued to lag. It was down around "8" and needed to be at least in the "13" to 15" range. I faced at least one more day in ICU and another twenty-four hours of not seeing the kids.

Maybe she could sneak the kids into ICU during the evening, Arlene said. The evening nurse had children and seemed to be sympathetic.

Later, when I was alone, I found myself reading an article from Men's Health, the magazine that Bryan and Larry had brought me. It claimed that getting up in front of an audience to speak was good for your overall health. Setting a goal on something to talk about stimulated the brain and got the creative juices flowing, the article said. Once you stood in front of a room full of people, you fed off all the energy in the room and received an adrenaline rush, too. The adrenaline produced was good for the endorphins in your brain.

As I read further, I thought about a club I had heard many good things about Toastmasters, the speaking club.

Grandpappy said I looked perplexed as I read the magazine.

"Oh, it's nothing," I said. "Just that this article was interesting. It was about a club I had been thinking about joining for awhile now. I think I would enjoy it, except for the time commitment."

"Well, how long have you been thinking about joining this club?" Grandpappy asked.

"I don't know, maybe a year or so. I had a friend who took me as his guest, and I really enjoyed it. Never went back, though. It's Toastmasters, by the way, the club for public speaking. I was just reading that speaking is good for your health."

"What has waiting to go back gotten you? Grandpappy asked me. "If you look back on that year and all of the experiences, think of all you have missed by not joining. You see, the next step is 'Now.' Do it now. Take action."

"I know, but the time…."

"Wait," he said, stopping me. "I know it takes effort and planning, but you have to understand, Jeff. What a man DOES is the real test of what a man IS. You see, CAN DO, WANT TO, WILL SOMEDAY, are all very different than DOING IT, TRIED IT, and DID THAT, which simply represent a better way of budgeting your time.

"Remember the goals you set for you and your family? You always need to move forward. There is an old Chinese proverb that says, 'Be not afraid of going slowly: Be only afraid of standing still.' Beginning is half the work. Once you start, you have to be disciplined to continue. It is, however, always worth the effort."

I told Grandpappy that I was a little apprehensive about trying Toastmasters, fearing that as a public speaker, I would be a flop.

"It doesn't matter," he said. "People put so much emphasis on winning, or being the best, that it is unhealthy. There are too many people who do not do the things in life they want to because they are worried about not being good. And so what if you are not that good. What should it matter as long as you try?

"It's just like the Little League parents who sit in the stands and gripe about the coach all day, yet those parents aren't there for all the practices or out there coaching themselves. Too many people sit on the sidelines of life. They watch and criticize the people out there trying because they didn't win or weren't the best, but they never take on the challenges themselves.

"When you are little and growing up, you are worried about what EVERYONE will say. As an adult, you still ask, what will THEY think or say? Even though no one has ever defined who THEY are.

"When you get as old as I am, you realize NOBODY was ever paying attention anyway. The problem then is you are too old to try on some of your dreams.

"Fulfilling dreams can and should be a habit. Yes, it takes work and effort, but all good things happen with action. Great men never wait for opportunities. They make them. They do not wait for the right equipment or better circumstances. They seize on whatever is at hand.

"You were put on this earth to succeed. That is what you are made to do best. But all accomplishment needs to have action. You can never reach the goal of your highest possibilities until you believe in your God-given power to do so. You need to be convinced that you are the master of your will, and the Creator has endowed you with strength to bend circumstances to aid you in the realization of your vision and your goals, whatever they may be. That is called learning. This is essential for a well-rounded happy individual.

"You must continue to learn. It is the biggest travesty of our time that we have convinced ourselves that education ends when you graduate from high school or college. By and large, people give up reading books or learning from tapes or TV. They are only worried about the latest TV entertainment show or movie, DVD or games. They quit trying new activities, because they are afraid they won't be good, or they are too old or don't have the time.

"It reminds me of a woman down the hall. Gladys is her name. She said to me just yesterday. 'Boy, I sure would like to go to college and get a master's degree in horticulture, but it will take eight years and I will be 53 when I graduate.'

"So I said, 'Well, just how old will you be in eight years if you do not go to college?'

"You see, life will always continue to go forward. Time will continue to march on, whether we take action or not. Some of the greatest achievements were from people more advanced in age who dared to try something they believed in.

"Colonel Sanders was in his sixties when he started Kentucky Fried Chicken. Ray Kroc was fifty-five when he started McDonald's. They all achieved because they took action. They took action toward a goal they felt strongly about and believed in. Did they succeed immediately? Of course not. The Colonel visited more than a thousand restaurants before a few would try his recipe. Ray Kroc had numerous failures before truly succeeding materially. The main thing is, they kept taking action. Just as you should do, Jeff.

"Always keep trying and always be positive. Play and enjoy what you try, and enjoy life as you go."

I was staring at the ceiling, thinking of all the actions I should take, when I realized Grandpappy was gone.

I rang the nurse for a shot of pain medicine. I had been listening so intently. Could be it was the raw truth smacking me around, but I felt sore and tired.

That probably explains why, in my dream, I was in a recliner at home. Buck, the man I worked for, was on TV showing how to construct a building. A sign on the structure said the company name and "your future" was here, if you wanted it. Buck kept turning toward the camera and asking me to help build the company. But I couldn't get out of my chair.

I grabbed the remote control and changed channels. Now Arlene, Ashley, Kayla and Sam were all playing on the beach, waving at me to join them. I still could not move.

I changed channels again, and I was sitting at a table in a room with twenty people. I knew them, but I couldn't even step in their direction. I realized it was a Toastmasters meeting. They were asking me to get up and speak, but I couldn't.

I changed channels one more time, and Arlene and the kids were at a gold mine. They were panning for gold and finding it. As they laughed, more gold appeared in their pans. They kept asking me to help them and share in the fun in the real riches of life, but I could not move.

I was paralyzed.

Chapter 7

It's in the Approach

I don't know how long I slept. But I was glad to see Grandpappy smiling back at me when I opened my eyes.

I apologized for falling asleep, but he insisted that I had been awake the whole time. Confused, I nonetheless told him about my dream of seeing everything I wanted on television, yet being unable to take any action to achieve it.

Grandpappy laughed, telling me I was simply missing the key success-driver behind action: enthusiasm.

"You can't build a fire when the fuel is wet," he said.

"Enthusiasm is faith in action; it is as simple as that. Nearly all of the great improvements, discoveries, inventions and achievements which have elevated and blessed humanity have been the fruits of enthusiasm. Most all people who are happy, joyful and fulfilled in life are people who have enthusiasm. It is the soul of a good character."

Once again he referred to an old proverb, this one Spanish.

"It says, 'He who loseth wealth loseth much; he who loseth a friend loseth more; but he who loses energy loseth all.' Just like we talked about the twin pistons of the human spirit, planning and purpose, well, enthusiasm is the twin brother of energy. The more enthusiasm you have toward the things that you do, the more energy you create.

"You need to put enthusiasm behind the action you take in all that you do. When you spend time at home, hang up the stress and troubles in a tree outside. Or just hang them on the door before you go into the house and forget about them. They will be there the next morning on your way out the door and, mysteriously enough, that bag of worries will be much less to deal with on a new day.

"When you go to work, be positive and enthusiastic, and you'll find that it will also help the people around you. Again, let me quote Andrew Carnegie, the great steel man in the early 20th century. He said, 'Give me a man with enthusiasm, and he can influence a plant of a thousand men, whether that enthusiasm is positive or negative.'

"Wow, does that say a lot. Do we think of the impact we have on those around us in the workplace? Everybody gives off energy with his or her presence. Their aura, if you will. The big question: Is that energy you are giving off POSITIVE or NEGATIVE?

"People of feeble action like to blame their misfortune on bad luck. They envy people who seem to climb the ladder of success, have all the nice things and are content. They say, 'Boy weren't they lucky? Didn't they get the breaks?'

"Actually, the breaks come, and opportunity knocks, as a result of enthusiastic action.

"You must be enthusiastic in all the things that you do. Also, see things through. Stick to everything you set out to do. Believe you were made for whatever task lies in front of you and tackle it as if no one can do it better. Learn to carry through, and you will be a hero. You will think better of yourself. Others will think better of you. The world admires a stern, determined doer. Become one, and people will see you in a new light."

He chuckled.

"Hey," Grandpappy continued, "what do you think the difference is between a man with enthusiasm and a man without it?"

I shook my head.

"About fifty thousand dollars a year," he said.

He then became more serious.

"You know I just can't say enough about enthusiasm, this dynamic characteristic. It is the compelling power that overcomes all difficulties and adversity, and enthusiasm all starts with you and you alone. You start with a smile, which by the way, is the only thing in the world that you can't break by cracking it."

He especially liked that one.

"Besides, why would you not want to smile? You are a child of God. Check the dictionary. It will tell you that 'enthusiasm' comes from two Greek words, 'en' and 'theos,' which mean 'in' and 'God.'

"When you plant enthusiasm into your actions, it is a feeling that is full of life.

"God wants you to be enthusiastic because you have Him in your life. When you put the enthusiasm and the action into your spiritual foundation and your relationship with God, you will be amazed at the sheer joy and happiness that you will almost attain.

"So put forth all of your energy and be enthusiastic putting your faith into action.

"Almost attain?" I asked quickly. "What else could there be except my relationship with God?"

"It's not your relationship, although that is important, of course. I'll tell you what is the most obvious, yet hidden nugget of God's wisdom later.

"But I must go. It's almost time for your dinner, and I know your wife, Arlene, will be back soon. We'll continue our discussion later. Good luck with the blood tests, and I sure do hope to see you get back in the main hospital."

I was wondering what 'nugget' Grandpappy was talking about as my eyelids shut out the light to the real world.

A dream soon followed.

I was running enthusiastically around an amusement park. Everybody in the park was walking around like a zombie, moving but not enjoying any of the activities. They were slow and lethargic. Their shoulders slumped. They shuffled their feet. It was the direct opposite of enthusiasm.

When I stood in line for the roller coaster, I started telling people about the definition of "enthusiasm," meaning "in God." They became excited and understood that enthusiasm would make every experience better and more productive and positive.

The problem was, it was taking way too long. I only spoke to about three people by the time I boarded the ride. How could I ever talk to all of these zombies in the park?

When I got off the ride, I was somehow at work, and I witnessed the same zombie-like behavior. The first person I told about enthusiasm was Buck, and our conversation returned him to normalcy. We went to lunch, where everyone in the restaurant was a zombie as well. We returned and walked through the office door onto a baseball field.

A bunch of little kids, mine included, were there. They were zombies, too. I realized it was going to be overwhelming to spread the word of enthusiasm effectively and wondered if I would ever be able to accomplish such a task.

Chapter 8

The Foundation

Grandpappy was right. I was tired and worried about this pending blood test.

The way I was living my life also troubled me. Everything the old man was saying seemed to ring true and make so much sense to me. But I couldn't keep from falling asleep again.

Then I was dreaming again.

I floated down into a room, vivid and massive in scale. It reminded me of a bar or restaurant, but it was just too big to be either one. I realized that I worked and ate meals there. The front wall to the room was all glass, and I could see beautiful scenery outside and people all around, especially kids.

Everyone outside was happy, and the kids were especially happy running around, shrieking with laughter and having no cares in the world. I then noticed that Arlene and the kids were out there. Arlene saw me, shrugged her shoulders and waved. I immediately looked for a way out, a way to reach them, but I could not find a door or window. She and the children were in a beautiful landscape, a park maybe. I was stuck in this huge, dingy, smelly room with a lot of other people I apparently worked with but did not know.

Then I noticed, over in a corner, a doorway with a sign where normally it would say "Exit." Instead, this sign said, "Way in Through Me." A man in a long, white robe stood underneath the sign. He was smiling in his robe, long hair and beard. He also wore sandals and held his arms outstretched, in a welcoming gesture. The man stood in front of the door, and one could not exit without seemingly passing through his body.

I went to the bar to order a drink, but there was nothing available. When I tried to eat food, I found I had no appetite. Why were all these other people drinking, eating and laughing, content to be in this room when it was obvious everything worthwhile was outside.

I looked toward the glass wall and noticed it had started to rain. Yet the rain was so beautiful. Arlene, Ashley, Kayla and Sam were all standing in the rain laughing, smiling and waving at me to come out and join them. Though afraid, I walked toward the man and the only doorway out. He continued to smile, too, while spreading his arms farther apart and motioning me to come to him. The closer I got, the calmer I became. I knew instinctively that everything was going to work out fine.

When I woke up, I found Arlene sitting near me, smiling as though she had some special secret she could no longer hold.

"I have a big surprise for you today … well, actually three of them," she said.

"Oh, yeah?" I said. "That wouldn't be three terrific kids, would it?"

"Yes, they are in the lobby. I have also spoken with the nurse, and when you finish your blood test and finish eating, she will let me bring them back."

"How are they holding up?"

"They had a great time at your sister's, but now that they are here, I think the gravity of the situation is setting in again."

She winced a little.

"But, hey, they are kids. They will be fine."

I was excited to see them, but the nurse came in first, loaded me into a wheelchair and pushed me down to the lab for some tests. They poked me for about a half-hour before taking me back for the hospital dinner, which reminded me of food I used to have on airline flights. But it didn't really bother me tonight, because the real dessert would be coming soon.

I knew that our nurse, Sandee, would be true to her word. She had been great, tending to me for most of my stay in ICU. I could just sense that she cared and empathized with my situation. She had had two grandparents die with heart attacks. She also had children and grandchildren, so I think she understood how much I needed to see my kids.

After Sandee took my tray away, she nodded to Arlene and could not contain her smile, despite the warning she readied to deliver.

"Listen," she said, "I could get in big trouble, so try to keep the noise level down when the kids come in, and I will see if we can get away with half an hour. And by all means, keep the curtain closed. Also, you may want to see if you can get up and walk back and forth in the room a little bit. Maybe your kids could help."

Two minutes later I heard:

"DAD!"

"DAD!"

"DAD!"

I received three hugs at the same time, though they were delivered as gingerly as possible.

They had a lot of questions and said things I wanted and did not want to hear.

"We missed you so, so much."

"When will you get out of here and come home?"

"Dad, are you going to be all right?"

Water pooled in my eyes.

"Are you going to die?"

"Of course not, don't be silly," I said. "However, my nurse, Sandee, told me that you three can help me with a little project I have to do."

I took it easy getting out of bed with Arlene and Denise's help. They stood in a corner as Ashley, Kayla and Sam steadied me as I walked slowly back and forth across the room. Jim kept the IV lines and oxygen tubes from being tangled and stepped on. We took these meaningful steps, to and fro, for about 10 minutes. I was amazed at how difficult it was and how much energy it sapped out of me.

Once I returned to the bed, the kids told me about staying with their aunt and uncle and all the things they had done, especially where they had gone out to eat.

Sandee soon stuck her head around the curtain with a motion that our time was up. But what good medicine it was.

I gave hugs all around and assured them that I would be back into the other part of the hospital in the next day or so. Jim and Denise stayed after Arlene and the kids had gone, and we talked for awhile. After they left, I settled in for what I expected would be a good night's sleep.

But before I did, I asked Sandee whether Elmer would be on duty that evening. Sandee still had no idea whom I was talking about.

"You just need to get some rest," she said. "If you feel uncomfortable, just push the call button."

After my visit from the kids, I slept great. Grandpappy greeted me when I opened my eyes the next morning. He asked how I had slept, and I explained that it was a good night, thanks to seeing my children.

"Yes, I am sure that did it," he said.

"You know," I said, "I had a fitful day yesterday and I am not sure why."

Grandpappy looked at me as if this was hardly a news flash.

"My guess is you feel uncomfortable about something," he said.

"Not really," I told him, "but I guess I have been thinking about work some."

"Really, why would work bother you now?"

"I don't know," I said. "I will be laid up for at least six weeks, and I guess I am wondering how things will get along without me."

"Are you afraid they will go bad or maybe go too good while you are gone?"

"Too good? What are you talking about?"

I was a bit defensive.

"Let me ask you," he said, "what are you afraid of when you are not there?"

"Nothing really. It is just that, you know, I have worked all my life and worked very hard to become a success, and I don't want heart trouble to take that away."

"Worked to become a success how?" he asked.

"You know, through books, listening to tapes, going to seminars and studying my craft, which is selling," I said, rather proudly.

"Well, you see there, that is why you are uncomfortable and why you are having fitful days. It would also explain your anxiety about what is coming next for you."

"What in the world are you talking about? How can working on improving my craft be a bad thing."

"Again, you misunderstand me," Grandpappy said. "I don't think it is a bad thing. I think it is a good thing. I just think you have everything in the wrong order, that's all. You see, if you could just learn this simple rule it would take away all of your stress, self-doubt, fear and worry. Not only about this but about everything else in your life."

"That sounds like a pretty tall order for one rule, Grandpappy." I said.

"No, here it is," he said. "Focus on your spiritual faith and your relationship with God and everything else will take care of itself. I can't make it any easier that than that."

"It can't be that easy to make your troubles go away," I protested.

"It does not make trouble go away," Grandpappy countered. Nobody ever said it did that. Spiritual people have problems just like you and I. They just have a better way to deal with them. They put their trust and faith in God.

"Let me give you an example of how God's word works. In the new King James Version of the Bible, the shortest chapter is Psalms 117; the longest chapter, Psalms 119. Psalms 118 lies in the middle. There are 594 chapters before Psalms 118 and 594 after it. Add those two numbers together and you have 1,188.

"Psalms 118:8 is the exact center verse in the Bible. Funny how that works, isn't it. So what does that mean? What is the center of God's word for us? It states the following, and I quote, 'It is better to trust in the Lord than to put confidence in man.'

"You see, faith does not get you out of trouble or hard times. It does not get you around trouble or hard times. It simply helps you get through them."

"That is pretty interesting," I acknowledged. "Is that really true, or are you just making this up as you go?"

"No," Grandpappy said, "I surely would not make up things about God. You don't have to. He is an amazingly loving and forgiving God who loves you like He does all people."

"So that's why he gave me the heart attack, is because he loves me, right?" I said with dripping sarcasm.

"Well, yes, I would say that is probably true," he said matter-of-factly. "As strange as it may seem, you had this heart attack for a reason. What that reason is I am not sure, but there is a reason to be sure. You see, God will not put you through any experience in your life without a reason or without giving you a seed of equivalent benefit in return. I don't know the reason, but he wants you to reflect and realize there is a reason. The key in your faith is to believe there is a seed of an equivalent benefit in it somewhere for you. A seed that will help you become a better or more well-adjusted person. This even holds true for the loss of a loved one. As hard as it is to understand, God has His reasons.

"Have you ever seen anyone do cross-stitching? You know, where they have the hoop and ring with the material stretched in the middle and thread every little stitch?"

"Yes," I answered. "Denise does it, and Arlene has done some. Why?"

"Life is a lot like that cross-stitching," he said, "If you were a little kid, or if you look up from the bottom of the cross-stitching, it would be just a massive tangle of different colored strings that made no sense whatsoever. Isn't that right?"

"Yes."

"Well, many of the things that happen to us we do not understand, and they do not make sense for what we want. We can't understand why God would put us through them. But when we die and go to heaven and we look back down on what our lives were, the cross-stitch version will be a beautiful picture. Every stitch or event will be in the perfect place, just as God has planned it.

"That is the importance of faith, to believe that we are making that picture every day. Even the suffering sometimes and doing things we feel are unnecessary.

"Jeff, spiritual faith is simply the most important thing you can have in life. With it, you have a good foundation when things are bad and something to be thankful for when things are good. You know, there are a lot of people who simply do not have a strong faith and it is so sad that they think life is about the money, the job, the title and the positions.

"As you nap today, think about your faith and your relationship with God. Put your faith in Him and pray. You might surprised what peace and comfort you can get from life and also the immense joy you will get from your loved ones when you realize that they too are a part of God's plan for you. The impact you have on them and they on you is a beautiful feeling. First you will get it, and then it will get you. And the thought of not going to church to worship the Lord would never cross your mind, and you will wonder what your life was like without faith."

"Thanks, Grandpappy," I said. "I will sleep on it."

I meant it, too.

"Well, get some sleep," he said. "You look tired, and I will see you soon."

In sleep, I returned to that same room with the glass wall. I apparently had everything in the room that I needed to survive: food, drink and work. Arlene and the kids were still outside, but the rain had stopped and it was still beautiful where they stood, dark and dingy on my side. The man still stood by the non-exit sign, but this time Grandpappy stood next to him.

He also was waving at me to walk through the door as he talked to the sandaled man, who was nodding in approval. This time, I was neither afraid nor hesitant. As I neared the door, I grew lighter in both body weight and step. I seemed to be floating toward the door but not going through it.

But I remained confident I would figure out how to go through the door. I knew in my heart that when I did, it would bring new meaning to everything. I kept floating closer to the door. Peacefully.

Chapter 9

The Building Blocks

Melissa, my day nurse, had great news when I woke up.

"Today, you will finally get your wish," she said. "You will be getting out of the IC unit."

The move would mean I could see my children more often, and Melissa knew that. She was as excited as I was.

"Great," I said, "when can we get that program started?"

"As soon as we can get you through breakfast and after the doctor comes in to see you," she explained. "I think we can do it soon afterwards, which, of course, is hospital-speak that means sometime before dinner tonight."

She hustled out to get her work done. The morning went by quickly. Arlene came in about 9. The kids could not enter, but everyone was excited when they heard the news that it was moving day for me.

Melissa turned out to be a prophet. It was just before dinner when they finally moved me to a regular room elsewhere in the hospital. I told Melissa what a great nurse she was and how I would miss her. I also asked about Elmer and if she had seen him that morning.

"Elmer? I don't know any volunteer named Elmer." she said.

"Everybody apparently calls him Grandpappy," I explained.

Again, she wore a blank expression. "Maybe he is just a night person and I have not met him yet," she added. "Is he new?"

"No, he said he had been a volunteer for awhile." I said.

I tried to recall the times that I had talked with him and remember what part of the day it had been each time. By then, Melissa and I were rounding a corner into my new room.

"DAD!"

"DAD!"

"DAD!"

All three kids gave me hugs and kisses again before backing up to allow me to transfer from wheelchair to bed. Needless to say, my thoughts about Grandpappy took a holiday while I was consumed with spending time with my family. Arlene and the children stayed until 8 p.m., when two nurses came in with a pint of blood for a transfusion.

They read numbers back and forth to each other so there was no mistake. Arlene packed up the kids, their books and coats. They fussed a bit a real sign that they were tired. It had been a trying week for them, too.

My family gone for the evening, I lay there with new blood dripping into my veins very slowly. I was pretty much burnt out on TV, so I stared out the window and watched a light snow coming down. I reflected on all that had happened in last few days. I think it finally started to sink in how serious this all was. I also realized how life, as I knew it, would have to change. I would have to exercise, reduce stress, eat better, know my goals, rely on faith. There was so much ahead of me.

Of course, I started thinking about the old man and all of the things he had taught me. It had been such a short time, yet he seemed like a wise, old friend. Guess who walked through the door then.

"Well, well, look what we have here," he said. "Looks like we are making big progress."

"Yeah, a couple of more days and maybe they let me leave this place," I said.

"That would be good. I know you are excited to get home to your family."

"But I will miss my lessons," I said. "How will I ever find happiness?"

I was half-joking. Half, because I really did want to find happiness. I just didn't want him to see how desperate I was.

"I don't know if you'll find happiness or not," Grandpappy said. "That will be up to you. You already have heard most of the secrets. All you are really missing are two pieces to the puzzle."

"Two?" I said. "It certainly doesn't seem like we have covered that much significant stuff. Are you sure?"

"Not only have we covered it, that 'stuff' is an acronym just so you don't forget.

"Let's recap. First, we have 'H' for health. It is the first step, remember?"

"Oh, yeah," I said. "I remember I was so groggy that I almost forgot, but that is about as plain as the nose on my face."

He continued.

" 'A' was for attitude. You remember, a can-do attitude, a never-give-up attitude!

" 'P' and 'P' were the twin pistons that drive the human spirit, remember? They stood for purpose and planning. In life, you have to know where you are going and have a good reason to go there. Those two will give you more drive and energy than anything else in the formula.

" 'I' was for independence. If you recall, you cannot be focused and happy carrying a load of debt on your mind all the time.

" 'N' was now. Take action. Don't wait. Don't procrastinate."

I found myself nodding as our previous talks came back to me.

" 'E' was enthusiasm," Grandpappy said, "and, of course, an important component that we talked about yesterday was 'S,' your spiritual faith."

"You left one out unless they have started spelling it differently," I said, proud of my spelling prowess.

A moment of silence followed, and Grandpappy noticed the puzzled look on my face.

"Are you all right?" he asked.

"Yeah, I was just trying to figure out the last letter, the second 'S,'" I said.

"Funny you should ask," Grandpappy said. "It is service."

"Service? What do you mean exactly?"

"Service to others," he said. "Helping other people. Helping people in need."

"To be honest with you" I said, "what I think about when people say you need to help and be of service are the people who start homeless shelters. People who take old race dogs and find them homes. People who do these lemonade stands to raise money and it becomes a regional or national thing.

"I just can't see myself doing something like that, and I don't have any ideas that could help that many people."

"No, no, no, that is not what I mean," Grandpappy said. "I mean, that is all good and well, but it is also rare. It is something that is more the exception than the rule. There is an old Mexican proverb that says 'Don't ask God for resources ask him to put you were the resources are.' What I am talking about is the people around you, the people you come in contact with every day. People like your family, your co-workers, your boss, and the people you go to church with. All these are people you are of service to, whether you realize it or not.

"When you really understand the last concept about God's being in control and guiding you to where you need to be to fulfill His purpose for you, then you are exactly where he wants you. You see, God does things differently than people. Don't you think your being a good father makes you of service to your kids? You give them a good role model. If you live a good Christian life, it is a shining example to those around you.

"Being a good husband is a good service to Arlene. The way you conduct yourself in doing the right things in life and in situations is a service to all those who you come in contact with. Your character.

"Let me give you an unusual example. Most of my life I ate lima beans when I would eat at a restaurant. Not because I liked lima beans that much, but because I watched my Dad eat them as a little kid and he liked them. It's not that I don't like them, but I think I ate them more because he did. I guess my point is, kids do not always listen to what you say, but they always watch what you do. Our actions are like throwing a stone in a pond. It ripples out to affect other people around us, whether our actions are good or bad."

"I get that, Grandpappy, but I thought God meant for us to be of service to everybody."

"Yes, that is right, too. Take your coaching those little kids on your ball teams. They look up to you whether you realize it or not. So what kind of service do you offer? Are you the type who yells at them if they lose or play poorly? Do you yell at the referees and maybe let a profanity or two slip? They are always watching how you handle things. What type of service do you give them? Is it a good example or a bad one?

"When you tell your kids to clean up their room, is the garage so messy you can't walk inside? When you tell them not to cheat or steal, do you take them to the restaurant and lie about their ages to save a dollar or two on the bill? These are the things they see.

"The same holds true for work or for church or anybody you come in contact with. What type of impression or service are you leaving? The interesting thing about how God works is lots of times we leave an impression on someone and we never realize the way we have affected that person.

"Let me ask you, have you ever sat around a room reminiscing with a group of friends about stuff that happened years earlier?"

"Of course, I have," I answered. "I think most people do all the time."

"When you have done that," he said, "have you ever retold a story about an event in your life, say, ten years earlier. You start to recount it with a couple of the primary characters in the same room. More than likely, there will be several different versions of the same event. Sometimes a person who was there barely remembers it, while you remember every little detail including the clothes you were wearing.

"That happens because it had a different impact on all of you. The problem is, you never know when your impact on someone will be a lasting one or not. My point is, when you interact with people it is important to be a Christian all of the time, not just on Sunday.

"That is what God meant to be of service. Do the best and be the best you can at all times. Does that mean you should not give freely of your time to help others? No. Does that mean you should not give freely of your talent to help others? No. Does that mean you should not share your treasure or money with those less fortunate? Absolutely not.

"But when you help a neighbor with a small chore. When you take an old friend to lunch. When someone has been through a tragedy and you're there for them to talk, to have a shoulder to cry on, so to speak. That is all service in God's eyes.

"Many people will say they don't know how to talk or deal with people facing a personal tragedy. Well, just saying you care and will pray for them will help tremendously. People know that you probably feel uncomfortable, but you made the effort. If you don't like talking to them, drop them a card. Not once, but again a couple of months later. Many times people are overwhelmed with an outpouring of sympathy and goodwill right after a tragedy. You can have a huge impact by remembering them two, maybe even three months later, as well. Don't just say you care and then forget about them. Remember, your actions speak loudly.

"God works in our life all the time, and every interaction can be a chance to be of service to your fellow man. So please don't get too hung up on the big events you read about all the time. Rather, focus on the people around you and how you can help them and just be there for them sometimes.

"Well, Jeff, I've got to get home, but good luck with the transfusion, and we just might see you before you go."

He headed out the door.

"Hey, Grandpappy, are you being a servant to me?" I asked with a smile.

"Well, sure, I am trying to be, but I guess you would have to make that determination."

"Yes, I think you are," I said. "I truly think you are. Thanks."

In my dream that night, I had returned to the huge room again. Only this time I was outside looking in. Nobody on the inside seemed to notice me, Arlene and the kids. However, it didn't matter. We were so happy, and the man in the white robe was on our side of the glass, too. I eventually noticed that I was wearing a black-and-white tuxedo, the kind a waiter might wear. I wasn't carrying around any drinks or food, but I did feel I was in a servant's role.

I looked at Arlene, and she wore a maid's uniform. On the outside, we all wore either a tux or a maid's outfit, and we were all serving each other. I told these people Grandpappy was right. It's the little things that matter. I looked at the man in the robe and sandals and there was Grandpappy, smiling and pointing at me. I nodded in his direction as my dream went to white.

Chapter 10

The Keystone

Grandpappy, sitting and reading the morning paper, greeted me immediately when my eyes opened. A bedside clock said it was 6:30.

"Wow, you are in early this morning," I said.

He had some interesting news.

"I plan to take a short vacation from this place after today, and you will, too, though I hope your break is a lot longer," he said. "You're going home this afternoon, if you hadn't heard."

"Where are you going?" I demanded. "I assumed you were a fixture here. And who told you I would be going home today?"

He ignored my last question.

"I'm just taking off for awhile," he said. "At my age, you need to do that. Maybe I'll read a little. Rest some. But I'm hoping I've made an impression. You should feel as though you have a good road map to finding the real happiness you want. The trick for you, as for everyone, is to be able to put the system into place and stick with it."

"You really think I'll find it difficult?" I asked.

"The discipline? Yes, I do. Mainly because we all get distracted and down on ourselves and find ourselves back on a roller coaster. You know, I think there are three other things. Characteristics, if you will. We need to do that are part of the formula but just don't fit into the main body. They demonstrate your maturity, spiritually and as an adult.

"First, stay humble. No matter if things are going well or poorly, humility is one of the most dynamic characteristics a person can possess. It says in Proverbs 18:12, 'Before destruction the heart of man is haughty, and before honor is humility.'

"Humility is a beautiful setting for the diamond of talents and genius. The mark of the truly successful man is absence of pretensions. He sticks to business, avoids all bragging and arrogance, makes no promises and goes the extra mile. He speaks in facts, not emotions.

"Modesty is the crowning ornament of a woman's beauty. Humility translates to sheer class. So whether you're a man or woman, humility is a key.

"Another thing to strive for: Don't be afraid to stay playful and childlike. Have fun in what you do. While we're taking life so seriously, we never stop anymore to run in the rain, climb a tree or go for a walk in bare feet.

"There is an old Chinese proverb that says, 'A truly great man never puts away the simplicity of a child, and you will find the two go together.' It says in Matthew 18:4, 'Whosoever, therefore, shall humble himself as this child, the same is greatest in the kingdom of Heaven.'

"I encourage you to watch and be like your kids more often. I am not talking about acting like juveniles, but I think you get my meaning.

Jeff, did I ever tell you the story of Bobby Dean, the man I first met back in the '40s?"

"No, his name has never come up."

"Bobby was a man who never had any self-confidence. He lost his parents and was kicked around from orphanage to orphanage as a child. When he grew up, he worked in a restaurant as a dishwasher. He lived in a boarding house over on Oak Street. One day he met and became friends with a man named Marvin. Now Marvin was a man who did Tarot cards and convinced Bobby that he was on the brink of seeing his life change dramatically for the better. In fact, Marvin told Bobby that in a previous life, Bobby had been the famous explorer, Marco Polo.

"Of course, Bobby did not believe him at first, but eventually Marvin persuaded him that everything he and his cards said was true. Once Bobby started believing he had the characteristics of someone else, he started doing better at work. Soon he was a cook. Shortly after that, he became the manager, and eventually he bought the restaurant. Within a few years, Bobby owned three restaurants and had long since moved out of the boarding house. He also got married and had kids.

"One day he was in his office when he read in the paper that his friend Marvin had been arrested and exposed as a fraud. Bobby could not believe it. He immediately began to panic. He started thinking his success was built on a lie, that he would very quickly go back to being a dishwasher.

"As his panic grew, he noticed a Band-Aid on his desk. For whatever reason, he focused on that Band-Aid and it led to a little poem. As he wrote down the last line, he knew to whom he owed his success. And he also knew one of the deepest secrets to being successful, happy and joyful in life. This is a critical element to have and to understand.

"Now, Jeff, I want you to remember this poem because it is the essence of what I am talking about:

What is it with a kid and a Band-Aid?
The greatest miracle cure conceived
For scrapes, bumps or bruises it does not matter which
This will fix it because they believe!
This plastic strip, believe it or not,
Spews magic from its very pores
If you're not convinced, watch it work

when a small kid takes a fall on the floor.
So to dream of the person you would like to be
Is to waste the person you are.
So chase your dreams forever, my friend,
No matter how near or how far!
For this old world goes round and round
And I am sure that you will find
There is no greater power on earth
Than the power of your mind.
So whatever challenge you face, wherever your place
Or how big our dreams may be,
Know in you heart and always BELIEVE
For you know of the power in me.
Always remember whatever you face
Adversities, dreams or despair,
You'll make it through just as you want
If the BELIEF in you heart is there.
So keep me around to remind you,
When you find yourself ever in doubt.
If a five-cent miracle can work for a child,
We big kids should figure it out.

"That poem says so much about what we lose as we age," Grandpappy continued. "A vast number of men and women, who are really capable of doing great things, do small things instead and live mediocre lives. They do not expect or demand enough of themselves.

"You see, a stream can not rise higher than its source. A great success must have a great expectation of self-confidence and persistent effort to attain it. No matter how great the ability or how smart or splendid the education, the achievement will never rise higher than the confidence.

"He can who thinks he can, and he can't who thinks he can't.

"This is an indisputable law. It does not matter what others think of you, of your goals, your dreams. Whether they call you a crackpot or a dreamer, you must believe in yourself. You forsake yourself when you lose your confidence. Never allow anybody or any circumstance to shake the belief in yourself. You may lose your property, your reputation, other people's confidence, but there is always hope for you as long as you keep a firm faith in yourself.

"Jeff, what I am telling you is that you must learn to do these things for me and yourself.

"Believe in your faith.

"Believe in your values.

"Believe in your abilities.

"Believe in your dreams.

"And above all believe in yourself.

"That is the final key, the foundation on which the whole system is built.

"So there. I've said my piece. It's time for an old man to go on vacation."

I thought I saw a few tears coming to his eyes.

"Hey, wait, will I not see you anymore?" I asked, and I moved toward the edge of the bed to stop him.

"You never know how things will work out," he said, "but certainly not for awhile."

"What about your phone number? I could call you after I get out of here and maybe we could meet for lunch. Or maybe you could come over for dinner and meet Arlene and the kids."

"No, I don't have a phone, but I will stay posted on your progress."

Then he was gone.

I was exasperated. And so tired. I soon fell asleep again.

Arlene and the kids were in the room when I woke up. Grandpappy was right. The doctor had told Arlene that I could go home that afternoon after lunch. I would be following, of course, strict rules about diet and exercise.

Checking out of the hospital took longer than expected. The kids watched cartoons on the room's television, while I caught up Arlene on all the things Grandpappy had taught me. We talked about having him over for dinner, but I confessed I had no idea where he lived or how to contact him.

Arlene went to the nurse's desk and inquired about this volunteer named Elmer, but again no one seemed to know him. I was confused and disappointed and thought to myself, was this anyway to run a hospital? But I also was desperate to get home.

I had been in the hospital seven days. I had nearly died, and I faced a long recovery. But those days in the hospital had been so enriching, too, thanks to an old man and his "system." I had a whole new outlook on life and how I wanted to approach it.

I didn't know who Grandpappy was. I knew only that I had met a special man.

Epilogue

18 months later

I was driving into the neighborhood and drinking in the sight of the manicured lawns, much as I had done eighteen months earlier.

In fact, I was thinking about that same night when I selfishly patted myself on the back and felt betrayed by the family's lack of understanding for my hard work. I cringed, remembering how I had shouted, stormed away to my office and symbolically locked them out.

When I reached home this night, I stood on the porch for a few minutes appreciating the difference Grandpappy had made in the life of me and my family.

I am not sure what or who he was. Arlene and I have talked about this more times than I can count. We have tried to find him. We tried for weeks to reach someone who knew him, but to no avail. Had I imagined him? Was he part of a recurring, drug-induced dream? Was he an angel sent from God? I doubt I will ever figure it out. I leave it to you for the answer and, if you have an idea, drop me a line and let me know.

This much I do know: Life for me and my family has changed drastically.

For one thing, as I arrived home now, it was 5:30, not 8. I would be in time for dinner, as I have been since the heart attacks. I don't stay at work late any longer, because I realize that my family is far more important. We eat dinner together, we read as a family, and we go for a walk as a family every night.

Once a week, we turn off the TV and have game night and just play board games and talk.

I am taking far better care of my health. Work still represents stress and pressure. I think everybody faces that to different degrees. But I have learned to leave work at work.

At home, we are busy with our budget and getting ourselves out of debt. The luxury car has been traded in for a used station wagon. It still looks good and runs good, but it has the best feature any car could have it is paid for.

I now spend a tremendous amount of time with the kids and with Arlene. Missing the children's school or sports functions is not acceptable. The kids no longer go to a private school, although we are very involved in their education. We know they are better served with the parent involvement on a daily basis.

We are writing down and planning goals that I never dreamed possible before we adopted our new system. What Grandpappy taught me has been a tremendous tool for bringing our family together and experiencing some of the most enjoyable times we have ever had.

Arlene, Ashley, Kayla, Sam and I set goals and make plans for our future. It is so gratifying to watch the kids achieve and build their self-confidence that way, and, yes, we are taking action with enthusiasm. It is truly amazing what we have accomplished is such a short time.

Probably the best part is my relationship with God and my spiritual faith. It has grown tenfold in the last few months, and I know it will continue to do so. I no longer look at service to others as such a daunting task, and I take it all one day at a time doing what I can do.

The amazing thing is, I do not worry about what other people think about my success. I am satisfied to be who I am and to be at home and love my family and embrace the love in those around me.

Grandpappy said that happiness is a state of mind when your thoughts are pleasant the majority of the time. I believe I have reached that point in life. I don't sense the void I felt in my life before the heart attacks. All of the possessions in the world will do you no good if you do not have happiness in your thoughts and joy in your heart.

I know I would not want to change a thing in my life now.

Ashley saw me standing on the porch.

"Hey, Dad," she yelled. "Time for dinner."

As soon as I walked into the house, Kayla asked, "Dad would you play a game with us after dinner?"

"Sure, what game are we going to play?" I asked.

"I know!" Sam shouted. "Let's play the game of LIFE."

I smiled.

"Yeah," I agreed. "Let's play the game of LIFE."

Printed in the United States
38208LVS00001B/124-156